Wonderful words

POEMS ABOUT READING, WRITING, SPEAKING, AND LISTENING
SELECTED BY *Lee Bennett Hopkins*
ILLUSTRATED BY *Karen Barbour*

SIMON & SCHUSTER BOOKS FOR YOUNG READERS
New York   London   Toronto   Sydney   Singapore

Acknowledgments

Thanks are due to the following for works reprinted herein:

Geoffrey Armour for "The Period" from *On Your Marks: A Package of Punctuation* by Richard Armour (McGraw Hill, 1969). Used by permission of Geoffrey Armour, who controls all rights.

Curtis Brown, Ltd. for "Let's Talk" by Rebecca Kai Dotlich, copyright © 2004 by Rebecca Kai Dotlich; "Listen" by Lee Bennett Hopkins, copyright © 2004 by Lee Bennett Hopkins; "Share the Adventure" by Patricia and Fredrick McKissack, copyright © 1993 by Patricia and Fredrick McKissack. First appeared as a National Children's Book Week Poem by The Children's Book Council. All reprinted by permission of Curtis Brown, Ltd.

Harcourt, Inc. for "Primer Lesson" from *Slabs of the Sunburnt West* by Carl Sandburg, copyright © 1922 by Harcourt, Inc. and renewed 1950 by Carl Sandburg; "Writing Past Midnight" from *A Lucky Thing* by Alice Schertle, text copyright © 1999, 1997 by Alice Schertle. Both reprinted by permission of Harcourt, Inc.

Harvard University Press for "1212" by Emily Dickinson. Reprinted by permission of the publishers and the Trustees of Amherst College from *The Poems of Emily Dickinson,* Thomas H. Johnson, ed., Cambridge, Massachusetts: The Belknap Press of Harvard University Press. Copyright © 1951, 1955, 1979 by the President and Fellows of Harvard College.

Lee Bennett Hopkins for "I Am the Book" by Tom Robert Shields. Used by permission of Lee Bennett Hopkins for the author.

Karla Kuskin for "Finding A Poem." Used by permission of the author, who controls all rights.

Lee & Low Books, Inc. for "Words Free as Confetti" from *Confetti: Poems for Children* by Pat Mora. Copyright © 1996 by Pat Mora.

Little, Brown and Company for an excerpt from "How to Learn to Say a Long, Hard Word" from *Speak Up* by David McCord. Copyright © 1979, 1980 by David McCord. By permission of Little, Brown and Company, Inc.

Ann Whitford Paul for "Word Builder." Used by permission of the author, who controls all rights.

Penguin Putman, Inc. for "The Dream" from *A Dime A Dozen* by Nikki Grimes. Copyright © 1998 by Nikki Grimes. Used by permission of Dial Books for Young Readers, an imprint of Penguin Putnam Books for Young Readers, a division of Penguin Putnam, Inc.

Marian Reiner for "Metaphor" from *It Doesn't Always Have to Rhyme* by Eve Merriam. Copyright © 1964, 1992 by Eve Merriam. Used by permission of Marian Reiner.

Heidi Roemer for "Night Dance." Used by permission of the author, who controls all rights.

To Daniel L. Darigan—
teacher of wonderful words
—L. B. H.

For David
—K. B.

SIMON & SCHUSTER BOOKS FOR YOUNG READERS
An imprint of Simon & Schuster Children's Publishing Division
1230 Avenue of the Americas, New York, New York 10020

Book design by Paula Winicur
The text for this book is set in Parango.
The illustrations are rendered in gouache on Arches 140 lb watercolor paper.
Manufactured in China

2 4 6 8 10 9 7 5 3 1

CIP data for this book is available from the Library of Congress.
ISBN 0-689-83588-4
Page 4 constitutes an extension of this copyright page.

CONTENTS

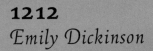

1212
Emily Dickinson

A word is dead
When it is said,
Some say.

I say it just
Begins to live
That day.

METAPHOR
Eve Merriam

Morning is
a new sheet of paper
for you to write on.

Whatever you want to say,
all day,
until night
folds it up
and files it away.

The bright words and the dark words
are gone
until dawn
and a new day
to write on.

WORDS FREE AS CONFETTI
Pat Mora

Come, words, come in your every color.
I'll toss you in storm or breeze.
I'll say, say, say you,
taste you sweet as plump plums,
bitter as old lemons.
I'll sniff you, words, warm
as almonds or tart as apple-red,
feel you green
and soft as new grass,
lightwhite as dandelion plumes,
or thorngray as cactus,
heavy as black cement,
cold as blue icicles,
warm as *abuelita's* yellowlap.
I'll hear you, words, loud as searoar's
purple crash, hushed
as *gatitos* curled in sleep,
as the last goldlullaby.

I'll see you long and dark as tunnels,
bright as rainbows,
playful as chestnutwind.
I'll watch you, words, rise and dance and spin.
I'll say, say, say you
in English,
in Spanish,
I'll find you.
Hold you.
Toss you.
I'm free too.
I say *yo soy libre,*
I am free
free, free,
free as confetti.

> *abuelita* (ah-bweh-LEE-tah): grandmother
>
> *gatitos* (gah-TEE-toce): kittens
>
> *yo soy libre* (YO SOY LEE-breh): I am free

14

HOW TO LEARN TO SAY A LONG, HARD WORD
David McCord

5.
Limicoline, **an adjective, describes**
some shore birds, like sandpipers—little tribes
that trot along the curvy line of foam
when tides are running out or coming home.
They skip, you know, like tiny clockwork toys
whose legs crisscross, crisscross, but make no noise.
Limicoline **means "living in the mud,"**
not in the *earth* **like turnip, beet, or spud:**
lim-
Mick-
a-
line.

There's something fresh and clean
about the *sound* **of it. See what I mean?**

WORD BUILDER
Ann Whitford Paul

Begin your new construction
with twenty-six letters.
Hammer *a* through *z* into words.
Pile your words like blocks
into sentence towers—
measure some tall,
saw others short.
Mortar each sentence
with punctuation,
then frame your sentences
into paragraph villages,
stack your paragraphs
into chapter cities.
Keep on building
words into sentences
sentences into paragraphs,
paragraphs into chapters
until you have created
a whole world of book.

I Am the Book
Tom Robert Shields

I'll be your friend,
  stay by your side,
  contradict you,
  make you laugh or teary-eyed
On a sun-summer morning.

I'll spark you,
  help you sleep,
  bring dreams
  you'll forever keep
On a dappled-autumn afternoon.

I'll warm you,
  keep you kindled,
  dazzle you
  till storms have dwindled
On a snow-flaked winter evening.

I'll plant in you
  a spring-seedling
  with bursting life
  while you are reading.

I am the book
You are needing.

SHARE THE ADVENTURE
Patricia and Fredrick McKissack

Pages and pages
A seesaw of ideas—
Share the adventure

Fiction, nonfiction:
Door to our past and future
Swinging back and forth

WHAM! The book slams shut,
But we read it together
With our minds open

LET'S TALK
Rebecca Kai Dotlich

About new robins
who appear
before winter
is through, the blue
of sky in July.
The turtle's shell.
Don't forget to tell
me how you've been.
Let's talk
of snow on mountains.
Summers in cities.
Pages.
Postcards.
Valentines.
Good times
we've had.
How it feels
to be sad.
Let's talk
about old dogs we love.
And speaking of love,
the turtledove.
Sit tight. Let's chat
all night.
About tomorrow,
about yesterday,
about people
who go away.
Let's name rivers.
Wish on stars.
Sit closer. Let's talk.
Tell me
how you are.

LISTEN
Lee Bennett Hopkins

Listen
to
soft-silences
stumbling
midst
loud-rumblings

now
and
then.

Hear
powerful
poundings
of
quiet,
hushed,

yet—

momentous sounds

    over
    over
    over

again.

FINDING A POEM
Karla Kuskin

Dig deep in you.
Keep everything you find.
Sketch the ever changing views,
dappled behind your eyes,
rustling in your mind.
Unlock the weather
in your heart.
Unleash a thousand whispers,
let them shout.
Then
when you feel
the presence of a poem
waiting to spring
to sting
within you,
bewitch it
into words
and sing it out.

THE DREAM
Nikki Grimes

Oh! To poet
like a laser,
pierce darkness
with one word!

WRITING PAST MIDNIGHT
Alice Schertle

insects drone . . . the night draws on . . .
I am writing a poem about a barn . . .

and my room is warm with the breath of horses
and dust from the loft runs in streams down the walls
and somewhere the sound
                          of sheep snoring softly
blends with the hum of computers
                          asleep in their stalls
bundled with bailing wire
                    stanzas
                    are stacked
                    to the ceiling

spiderwebs anchor the edge of my desk to the floor
a small gray verse runs squeaking down one of the rafters

just as the moon floats in through the double barn door

NIGHT DANCE
Heidi Roemer

Haiku dart about
like hummingbirds—asleep I
dream—exquisite words.

PRIMER LESSON
Carl Sandburg

Look out how you use proud words.
When you let proud words go, it is
   not easy to call them back.
They wear long boots, hard boots; they
   walk off proud; they can't hear you
   calling—
Look out how you use proud words.

THE PERIOD
Richard Armour

Fat little period, round as a ball,
You'd think it would roll,
But it doesn't
At all.
Where it stops,
There it plops,
There it stubbornly stays,
At the end of a sentence
For days and days.

"Get out of my way!"
Cries the sentence. "Beware!"
But the period seems not to hear or to care.
Like a stone in the road,
It won't budge, it won't bend.
If it spoke, it would say to a sentence,

"The end."